Profitable Fowls and Eggs

How To Make Money From Poultry

by Harrison Weir

with an introduction by Jackson Chambers

Self Reliance Books

Get more historic titles on animal and stock breeding, gardening and old fashioned skills by visiting us at:

http://selfreliancebooks.blogspot.com/

Introduction

I am pleased to present yet another title on Poultry.

This volume is entitled "Profitable Fowls and Eggs and How To Make Money Of Them" and was published in 1873.

The work is in the Public Domain and is re-printed here in accordance with Federal Laws.

As with all reprinted books of this age that are intended to perfectly reproduce the original edition, considerable pains and effort had to be undertaken to correct fading and sometimes outright damage to existing proofs of this title. At times, this task is quite monumental, requiring an almost total "rebuilding" of some pages from digital proofs of multiple copies. Despite this, imperfections still sometimes exist in the final proof and may detract from the visual appearance of the text.

I hope you enjoy reading this book as much as I enjoyed making it available to readers again.

Jackson Chambers

COCHIN CHINA HENS.

JAMES FLETCHER, ESQ.,

OF

CHILTON, BUCKS,

THIS LITTLE HANDBOOK

IS

Inscribed

BY

HIS FAITHFUL FRIEND,

THE EDITOR.

PUBLISHERS' PREFACE.

——————

The great interest taken by the public, and by ladies especially, in the rearing and profitable treatment of fowls, has induced us to publish this valuable little treatise in our series of Champion Handbooks. The text is principally from the pen of the well-known author of the "Poultry Book" and "Profitable Poultry," with such additions as the nature of the work now issued seemed to require. The whole may, we confidently believe, be accepted as a trustworthy guide by any poultry farmer or amateur henwife.

58, Holborn Hill, E.C.

CONTENTS.

CHAPTER I.

CHAPTER II.

CONTENTS.

CHAPTER III.

CHAPTER IV.

CHAPTER V.

PROFITABLE FOWLS AND EGGS.

CHAPTER I.

FOWL HOUSES AND FOOD FOR FOWLS.

THE question is very often asked, what are the best fowls to keep? If the person who asks the question does not state where he is going to keep his fowls—whether they are to have a free range over grass fields, or to be shut up in a small space, and, also, whether they are to be kept chiefly for the sake of their eggs, or for chickens for the table—it is impossible to answer such a question satisfactorily.

One kind or breed of fowl will do well in a confined space, where another breed would not answer.

One variety requires a sandy or chalky soil—another will succeed on one of clay, where the first would die.

Some breeds are remarkable for the vast number of eggs they produce, and others for the plumpness and rapid growth of their chickens.

Some varieties, again, fly like pheasants, and know not bounds, whilst others cannot leap over a fence three or four feet in height.

Therefore, it is evident that the circumstances in which the fowls are to be kept, and, also, whether numerous eggs or large chickens for the table are chiefly required of them, must be taken into consideration in determining what is the breed best suited for any particular situation. I shall, however, first speak of the fowl-house, and of the run where the birds are to be kept, before describing any of the particular varieties.

THE FOWL-HOUSE.

For a small number of fowls, any dry out-house will answer, provided it has no windows or doors left open to the cold east or north winds. In this house there must be perches for the fowls to roost upon.

These perches should not be placed high from the ground; for if they are, the fowls injure themselves very much when they fly down, often coming with so much force against the ground, as to break the projecting part of the breast-bone; and if the fowls are heavy, they also injure their feet, and thus become lame and useless.

The perches should be very much broader than they are usually made; for, when narrow and sharp-edged, the young birds that roost on them are almost certain to have their breast-bones pressed in, and made crooked by the narrow edge—an evil which is avoided by the perches being made three inches in breadth, with the edges rounded off, so that the bird's claws can curve round them.

To remove the droppings which fall below the perches, either of two plans may be followed. If a loose board is laid along under each perch, it may be lifted out of the fowl-house every morning, the refuse removed with a spade, and the board returned.

This is an admirable plan, and one which keeps the house clear and wholesome. Or sand or dry ashes may be strewn under the fowl-roost, and removed daily.

If the house is closely built, and several fowls are kept, there must be some means adopted for giving them fresh air; for they will soon become unhealthy if kept in a close, ill-ventilated roosting-place. But it should be remembered that fowls do not like a draught; and, if they are exposed to one, often catch a troublesome and infectious disease termed the croup.

It is very important that the fowl-house should be dry; for if fowls are compelled to roost in a cold, damp house, they are never free from disease.

The pattern or design of the poultry-house is of very little importance. I have kept and reared the finest fowls in all sorts of out-of-the-way places—an unused pig-sty, a stall in a stable, an old garden tool-house, or any such place will do, provided that it is kept clean, and that it is dry, and not liable to draughts of cold air.

The nesting-places are an important consideration in a fowl-house. The common plan of putting them up in rows on shelves, like what are called pigeon-holes in a counting-house, is the worst mode possible; for, from being so closely crowded together, the nests cannot be readily cleaned; and when the hens are sitting, they swarm with fleas and other parasites to such an extent that the fowls have no peace or rest in them, and so get irritable, and leave or break their eggs.

Then there is another great disadvantage arising from the nesting-places being all alike, the fowls are apt to mistake one nest for another, and a sitting-hen will often go into the next box, and leave her eggs for so many hours that they fail to produce chickens.

The best nesting-places are those that are perfectly distinct from one another, and that admit of being taken out and cleaned thoroughly when the hen has done sitting.

Nothing answers better than the round bushel or half-bushel baskets that are employed to send peas, beans, and other vegetables to the London markets. These may be put down in any place in the fowl-house that is convenient. Each one should be about half filled with coal ashes or loose earth, and then some short bruised straw put on the top. This is readily hollowed into a perfect nest, and is much better than a large quantity of straw or a flat board.

SITTING AND HATCHING.

When a hen sits in one of these baskets, she can at any time be covered over with a coop, so as to prevent other hens going into the same nest to lay—a circum-stance that generally leads to fighting, and, consequently, to the destruction of the eggs. As soon as the chickens are hatched, the basket should be taken out of the fowl-house, the straw and ashes or mould thrown out, and the basket washed, so as to get rid of the fleas, &c., with which it is apt to be infested.

June is the best month for hatching.

It is always the best plan to allow a hen to sit in the same nest in which she has been in the habit of laying, as there is usually a good deal of trouble and uncertainty in getting a hen to sit steadily in a strange nest.

When a hen becomes *broody* or wants to sit, she shows her desire by remaining on the nest, and by a strange clucking noise she makes in the place of her usual note. To ascertain whether she is likely to sit steadily, it is usual to give her three or four nest-eggs to sit on for a day or two. If she is found to sit well, the eggs she is to hatch should be placed in the nest when she leaves it to feed, and the nest-eggs taken away. The day on which the eggs are given her should be carefully noted down, and, if convenient, two hens should be sat on the same day, for a reason that will appear presently. The eggs for setting should be as fresh as possible, for if more than fifteen or twenty days old they do not hatch so readily as when fresher. If a friend who has a good breed of fowls offers you a sitting of eggs, you may safely accept them. They will hatch none the worse even if they have to be sent one or two hundred miles, provided they are properly packed in a hamper or basket with plenty of hay which is tightly pressed down, so as to prevent them shaking one against another. If you know an egg merchant, you may ask him for a dozen of the largest and freshest eggs from a chest from Normandy, and you may obtain a number of the large, useful, though not very handsome, breed, termed Crêve Cœurs; these are the celebrated French table fowls, that lay as large eggs as our Spanish, and are as plump and heavy as our Dorkings.

Do not put too many eggs under the sitting hen; all should be covered, not only by her feathers, but should be in contact with the naked skin of her breast. Thirteen or fourteen will be found quite sufficient for a large hen, even during warm seasons of the year.

The sitting hen should be well fed with barley when she comes off to feed, having as much food given to her as she will eat, and she should always have a heap of dry ashes or dust to roll in, so as to enable her to get rid of her fleas.

After the hen has been sitting for seven or eight days, you may examine the eggs, to see if they contain chickens. This is best done at night. To do this, take into the fowl-house a lighted candle and a basket with a little straw to receive the eggs. Put your hand gently under the hen, and take out one egg or two. Shade the candle from your eye with the left hand, making a ring by bringing the tip of the thumb and fore-finger together. Hold each egg in succession against this ring, so as to allow the light to shine through the centre of the egg. Those eggs that have chickens in will appear perfectly dark, except a clear space at the larger end; those eggs that are clear, and that look as if they were filled with melted wax, through which the light can shine, are useless, and should be taken away. After having examined all the eggs, replace the good ones under the hen. The advantage of setting two hens on the same day is, that if many of the eggs are clear, the whole batch can be given to one hen, and a fresh lot to the other.

After the hens have been sitting twenty days, some of the chickens begin to chip the shell. On this day the hen should not be disturbed. On the twenty-first day, that is the same day three weeks that the eggs were put under the hen, all the chickens will be hatched. Many persons take away those first hatched, and put them in a basket with flannel by the side of the fire. This is a very useless plan—the hen and chickens had much better be left alone. When undisturbed, the hen will not leave the nest till the twenty-second day, and then all the chickens will be found quite strong and able to run. On no account should the young chickens be crammed with food; until they are about thirty hours old, they do not require any other nourishment than the yolk of the egg from which they are hatched.

This passes into the inside, and nourishes them until they are sufficiently strong to run about and seek other food.

FOOD FOR CHICKENS.

The most convenient food for young chickens consists of whole grits; but their diet should be varied as much as possible. Coarse oatmeal, mixed into a crumbly mess with milk or water, chopped hard-boiled egg, or curd, are very useful; but the food on which young chickens make the most rapid and healthy progress is the supply of grubs, insects, small worms, ants' eggs, and other animal substances that the hen obtains by scratching.

Some persons say that the hens roam too much when they are not cooped, and weary the chickens; but if the hen is well fed, there is no danger of her wandering so far as to tire the chickens.

Having spoken of the fowl-house, I must now say a few words respecting the run or range provided for the birds.

THE RUN.

Fowls never do so well as when they can wander unconfined over a free range of grass or coppice, or scratch for their food in straw or manure heaps. Under these circumstances they obtain a great amount of food, and, consequently, cost much less to keep than when they have to be entirely fed by hand. And there is also the great advantage that the variety of food obtained in this way, conduces to their health and condition; so that their hardihood is far superior to that of fowls kept in a confined space, and the number of the eggs proportionately increased.

But still, fowls may be kept with advantage in a confined space, provided the most scrupulous cleanliness is employed, the house cleaned out daily, and the run often swept and gravelled.

The great mistake usually committed by persons who keep fowls in a small space, such as a back garden, is, that they attempt to keep three or four times the number that the place will accommodate.

I have now in a small stable-yard, quite open to the sun and air, and paved with coarse stones, one cock and three hens; the latter have been laying constantly for several weeks, and are in the most perfect health and condition, although the size of the yard is only six yards by eight; but the health of the birds is preserved by the roosting-place being kept sweet and clean, and the yard constantly swept. Then, in order to supply the green food natural to birds, all the waste garden stuff, such as cabbage-stumps, turnip-tops, &c., is thrown in for them to scratch and peck at; a spadeful of mould, full of worms and small stones, is often thrown in it, and the birds are fed with barley and all the house scraps, such as boiled potato-peelings, bones, crumbs, &c. Now, if I were to place eight or ten fowls in this space, it would become overcrowded, and the birds would soon get out of condition, and cease to do well.

FOOD.

Fowls require *warmth-giving food*, as starch-rice, the solid part of potatoes, &c.; *flesh-forming food*, as the gluten of wheat, oatmeal, peas, barley; and *fat-forming food*, as the yellow variety of Indian corn, and other things containing oily and fatty matters. These must be given in combination, not singly.

Grain forms, naturally, the principal food of poultry of all kinds. *Barley* is the best, as it contains a larger amount of flesh and fat-forming material. Next comes *oats*, which are to be given more sparingly, in consequence of the quantity of husks; but in the form of oatmeal it is highly nourishing and fattening, especially for Cochins and Spanish fowls. *Wheat* stands in rather less request; it is more expensive, and not more nutritive. *Rice* is useful only in the making of bone, and should, therefore, be given only in small quantities, except as a variation to richer food. Boiled rice is a capital food for chickens when taken in conjunction with barley and *buckwheat flour*, or *millet*, both of which are very nutritious. Bran, pollard, malt-dust, and middlings, are capital additions to the food of fowls.

The following *cooked food* is one that I can strongly recommend, as well adapted for fattening all kinds of poultry :—

"A quantity of middlings, with or without half its bulk of barley-meal, or a corresponding proportion of malt-dust, is placed in a coarse red-ware pan, and baked for about an hour in a side oven, or until the mixture is thoroughly heated throughout; water is then poured in, and the whole stirred together until it becomes a crumbling mass; if too much water is added, the mixture becomes cloggy, a defect which is easily remedied by stirring in a little dry meal. The advantage of this method is that the food is prepared with scarcely any trouble, and there is no fear of its being burnt, as in boiling. Sometimes the barley-meal is omitted, and the baked middlings mixed with rice which has been previously boiled. This mixture forms a good stock food for old fowls, a liberal supply of grain being given during the day. I have found that since its adoption they cost less in food, and that they are in equally good, or even in better condition, than when fed on an unlimited supply of grain alone. Should the convenience for baking not exist, it will be found more desirable to scald the middlings and meal with boiling water than to mix them with cold.

"If grain of any kind is broken or crushed, it should only be done shortly before use, unless it is thoroughly kiln-dried; for when this is not done, the grain, from the moisture it contains, soon becomes musty, sour, and unwholesome. Inferior samples of grain contain so large a proportion of husk that they are not desirable, and if regarded with reference to their nutritious properties, the best will be found the cheapest."

In the winter, when worms are scarce, fowls require a little *animal food* supplied to them. The best sort is fresh beef or mutton, chopped up small. I strongly condemn the use of tallow-chandler's greaves, as in every way injurious.

Water.—A daily supply of *fresh water* is indispensable. A cheap and capital drinking-fountain for fowls is made with an earthenware jar and a flower-pot saucer. Bore a small hole in the jar about an inch from its edge, fill the jar with water, put the saucer on the top, then turn both upside down. The water will be found to flow into the saucer to the height of the hole, and continue to flow till it is all exhausted.

There are few places where a cock and three or four to half a dozen hens cannot be kept to profit. The back yard of a town or suburban house will answer very well, provided it is open to the sun.

In such places as these, however, it will never be found desirable to attempt to rear chickens, consequently varieties should be kept that do not want to sit. For these confined town localities, no breed answers better than the Spanish.

CHAPTER II.

PROFITABLE VARIETIES.

SPANISH.

THIS well-known variety originally came, as its name implies, from Spain, and it was carried by the Spaniards to Holland at the time they had possession of that country, consequently good fowls of this breed are to be found there also.

In England, especially near London, the Spanish is a favourite breed. They stand a town life well, and their dark plumage does not show the dirt. As table-fowl, their long blue legs are rather against them, but as producers of numerous large fine eggs, they are most valuable. They rarely show any desire to sit, but go on laying all the year round, except at moulting time in the autumn. Hence, when chickens are required, their eggs must be hatched by hens of other varieties. The characters of the Spanish breed are very well marked. Their colour is a fine lustrous black, which should be without a suspicion of lead white or any other colour. Their legs are long, and the gait and courage of the cocks striking and majestic. The combs, which are very long and single, should be erect in the cocks, and in the hens should fall over to one side. Their most striking peculiarity consists in a white ear-lobe, of large size. This whiteness in first-rate fancy specimens extends over the whole face; but in general the face has more or less red above the eyes. As far as regards the production of eggs, the red-faced birds are as valuable as those with countenances entirely white, but as show birds at the exhibitions, the slightest blush of red would be fatal to any chance of success.

The chickens of the Spanish breed are remarkable for the length of time they take to produce their plumage, hence they run about for a long period with naked legs and necks. It is, therefore, not desirable to hatch them

except in the most favourable time of the year, unless especial conveniences exist for their protection.

To conclude my account of this variety, I may contrast their advantages and disadvantages.

The Spanish are a fine handsome breed; the contrast of colours in their black plumage, red combs, and white faces, is striking; they lay numerous large eggs and are adapted to a town life or confined space; their disadvantages are that they are too leggy to be first-rate fowls, that they do not sit, and that during autumn and early winter their long moult interferes with their laying. In many respects their merits far outweigh their faults, and they will always be favourites with many breeders.

The *Minorca* is a plump-bodied variety of the Spanish, with lustrous black plumage. The hens are good layers and not bad sitters.

GAME FOWL.

Of the game birds there are several varieties as to colour, but agreeing as to other characteristics.

In size, all game fowl should be of medium weight, very heavy birds never possessing that beautiful symmetry and grace which characterize the best birds of moderate size. First-rate game cocks rarely reach six pounds, and under four pounds for the hens should always be the size aimed at by the breeder.

The form of a game cock is difficult to describe, as there is no one part that is prominent, but all the parts are, as it were, combined into one harmonious well-proportioned whole.

The plumage should be hard, firm, and glossy; the tail well arched in the cock, and forming a large fan in the hen: the wings large, and carried close to the sides. The legs in the game cock are very fleshy and of great strength. The neck should be long, arched, and as the breeders term it, "reachy." The head in both sexes is unquestionably more beautiful than that of any other fowl: it is small, thin, long, and graceful as that of a greyhound, yet all appearance of weakness is taken

from it by the massive stoutness of the well-curved beak. The eye is large, full, and exceedingly brilliant; the comb small, thin, and quite erect. The spur in well bred birds is exceedingly dense and sharp, and even the hens are not unfrequently well-spurred.

Game fowl have been for many generations bred for the purpose of fighting; consequently all the efforts of the breeders have been directed to rearing birds that were the most active, powerful, and courageous—hence the present elegance and beauty of the race.

The most common breed of game fowl are those

known as the Black-breasted Reds, or, as they are generally termed for shortness, Black Reds. The cocks of this variety have the breast, thighs, and tail bright glossy black, the neck, back, and saddle red, and the wing-feathers bay, with a deep steel-blue bar across the wing.

In what are termed the Brown Reds, the breast of the cocks is mottled with brown, and the wing-feathers are dark, and not bay. It is strange that the hens of this brown-breasted breed are much darker in colour than the hens of the black-breasted cocks. This fact seems only known to practical breeders, for it is a common circumstance at poultry-shows to see black-red cocks in the same pen with brown-red hens, and *vice versâ*—a mistake of the exhibitor that is fatal to the remotest chance of success in winning the prizes.

In the variety called Duckwing Game, the cocks have usually a straw-coloured neck and saddle, deepening to red. The wing-feathers are light, and these, contrasting with the steel-blue bar across the wing, give rise to the name of Duckwing, from the close resemblance to the wing of the wild duck.

In addition to these varieties, there are Pure White Game, Pure Black, and a variety called Piles. In this latter breed, the cocks should be white where a Black Red bird is black, and red where he is red. As Piles may be produced by breeding from a black-red cock and a white hen, they are not held in such general estimation as a good black or brown-red, or as Duckwings.

All persons are aware of the courageous character of the game cock, and its tendency to fight to the death. This, however, is not found so great a disadvantage in keeping them as might be supposed; for as the young grow up, the old bird remains master over all, and he rarely permits any serious fighting between his sons, for if they begin he joins in, and soon reduces them to subjection. In fact, the young ones brought up in one yard may be kept together very well, one being always regarded as master; but if they are parted for a few days and then are brought together again, the result is a combat which may be fatal to one or even both.

However much it may shock some persons' ideas on the subject, there can be no doubt but that fowls in a wild state were created so as to fight: they have sharp-pointed natural spurs, which are sufficiently strong to be driven into the brain of an antagonist, and so kill him.

In fact, it is not very long since that a little child was killed by a Spanish cock, and I have got a mark on my own cheek where a game cock struck his spur quite through into my mouth. In fighting, the birds stand with the points of their beaks together, both raising their heads at the same time, and then they suddenly leap up into the air with a bound, striking against one another with a force that causes them to be thrown back with violence. The object of each bird is to leap suddenly above the other, so that it can strike with the spur from above. If one cock succeeds in catching hold of its adversary with its beak, it has a great advantage; for, forcing the head down, it leaps above, and drives one or both spurs deeply into the foe.

To prevent this advantage, game fowl are always *dubbed* or *trimmed:* that is, the comb and gills are cut off. This proceeding may appear cruel; but in reality it prevents a much greater degree of pain if the animal ever gets engaged in a combat, and consequently the plan is followed by all keepers and breeders of game fowl. As this has, therefore, to be done, I had better describe the mode of doing it properly, and with the least amount of suffering to the bird.

To take off the comb, a pair of sharp, thin, but strong scissors are required. Pressing these close to the head at the back of the comb (whilst an assistant holds the bird securely), they are then closed, and the comb cut off from the back to the front. The wattles or gills should be taken off at the same time, the bird being held securely, and each one removed with one cut of the scissors. Care should be taken to leave the band of skin between the wattles, otherwise a large wound is produced. This may be best done by simply cutting off each wattle without pulling it, merely letting it lie between the blades of the scissors as the head is turned up for the operation. The folds of red skin, near the ear-holes, which are termed the ear-lobes or deaf-ears by fanciers, should not be removed at the same time, but after the other cuts have healed. When a game cock has been well dubbed, his appearance is certainly much improved. The head becomes snaky, and the large eye, expressive of enduring courage, looks far more prominent and lustrous than before. At about the age of six months is usually the time at which this operation is performed.

With regard to the merits of the game breed in a

profitable point of view, when fowls have to shift largely for themselves, to seek part of their own food, and to rely on their own resources, there is no breed that does better than the game. Cocks and hens are alike courageous, and will fight desperately in defence of their young. The hens are exceedingly good sitters, and are unequalled as mothers. As egg producers, of course, they do not produce as large a number as those hens that, like the Spanish, the Hamburghs, and Polish, never sit.

For table use, the chickens are unsurpassed in the goodness of their flesh, but for selling in the market as table fowl, they have one or two drawbacks—that is, they are not as large as the Dorking or Surrey breed, and as the legs are almost always coloured, they are not quite so highly esteemed for boiling by some over-fastidious persons.

Nevertheless, taking all circumstances into consideration—their beauty, their self-reliance, their power of seeking a great portion of their own food, their admirable qualities as sitters and mothers, as well as their extreme goodness as table-fowl, it is difficult to recommend a better breed for those places where they are suited. Let me, however, caution my readers not to attempt game fowls in a confined space. If you cannot give your fowls a large or almost unlimited run, where there is grass and herbage for them to pick, and insects to be sought for and obtained, then do not try game fowl.

All their beauty depends on their being in high condition, so that their plumage should be lustrous, and their carriage the very *beau ideal* of grace and elegance.

This high condition game never reach except where they have a large grass run; so that those who have a confined space should cultivate another breed. For this purpose I can recommend none better adapted than the Spanish. Perhaps, however, some would prefer another variety. If so, let them try the Cochins, which also have their advantages, and, of course, their disadvantages.

COCHINS.

The great advantage that the Cochin breed offers

over every other arises from the fact that they lay better in winter than any other breed. Young Cochins of seven to eight months old begin to lay, if they are well fed, quite irrespective of the season or the temperature, and hence they are most valuable as layers in winter, when eggs are scarce and consequently valuable. Another great recommendation of Cochins is that they may be confined readily by a fence three feet six inches high. This is often a circumstance of great convenience. Cochins, again, are as hardy as any variety of domestic fowl. They hatch well, being very good mothers, and the chickens are so robust that they can be reared in almost any situation. Their disadvantages are, that, being of large size, they eat more than such smaller fowls as game, and although they weigh very heavy, they are not first-rate birds for the table. Their skin and fat are yellow, and look badly when the fowls are boiled, and there is not so much flesh on the breast as in game, and those breeds that use their wings in flight.

Nevertheless, their domesticity, their valuable egg-producing powers in winter, the ease with which they are confined, and their hardihood, justly render them favourites with many, and they are, consequently, never likely to be without their admirers.

The characteristics of good Cochins are size, shortness of leg, fulness of plumage, a certain square angularity of shape that contrasts strikingly with the slim elegance of the game fowl. The colour of Cochins varies : the most general colour is buff, then there are the partridge and grouse-coloured birds, and pure white. Formerly black Cochins were exhibited, but these seem to have lost their admirers, and are now rarely, if ever, seen. (*See* Frontispiece.)

BRAHMA POOTRAS.

The fowls known by this name are, in fact, grey Cochins crossed with the buff Shanghae. I have before stated, and I now repeat, that for stock purposes they are worthless; as they are leggy, with a remarkable tendency to accumulate internal abdominal fat, or "go down behind," as it is called, a state of health which leads almost certainly to irregularity in the egg organs. Nevertheless, they are hardy and not unhandsome.

DORKINGS.

For table purposes there are no fowls so profitable as Dorkings, though they are not particularly good layers. The favourite bird of the old fanciers was the rose-combed white Dorking, "which," says Mr. Brent, a thorough good judge, "is the only true, pure fowl." It is of good size, compact, and plump, with a short white neck, five toes, a full rose comb, a large breast, and plumage of spotless white. "The practice," Mr. Brent goes on to say, "of crossing with a game cock was much in vogue with the old breeders, to improve a worn-out stock, which, however, would have been better accomplished by procuring a fresh bird of the same kind, but not related. This cross shows itself in single combs, loss of a claw, or an occasional red feather, but, what is still more objectionable, in pale yellow legs, and a yellow circle about the beak, which also indicates a yellowish skin. These are faults to be avoided. As regards size, the white Dorking is generally inferior to the Sussex (coloured fowl), but in this respect it only requires attention and careful breeding.

"The Dorking is an excellent farm-yard fowl, being a good layer, a close sitter, and an attentive mother; the chickens grow rapidly, and are *excellent* for the table. The pure white Dorking may truly be considered as fancy stock as well as useful, because they will breed true to their points; but the Gray Sussex, Surrey, or coloured Dorking, often sport. To the breeders and admirers of the so-called 'coloured Dorkings' I would say, continue to improve the fowl of your choice, but let him be known by his right title; do not support him on another's fame, nor yet deny that the rose comb or fifth toe is essential to a Dorking, because your favourites are not constant to those points; the absence of the fifth claw to the Dorking would be a great defect, but to the Sussex Dorking it is my opinion it would be an improvement, provided the leg did not get longer with the loss."

The principal drawback to the Dorking is the delicacy of the chicken; but for persons who rear fowls in order to make money of them, they are invaluable for tenderness and delicacy of flavour.

The *Coloured Dorking* is much in favour with many. It grows large and full, and shows well at any exhibition of cottage produce. Mr. Bailey, a good judge of Dorkings, gives the following instructions for the selection of pairs of these fowls for show :—" One of the most popular colours for hens in the present day is that known as Lord Hill's. The body of these birds is of a light slate-colour, the quill of each feather being white; the hackle is that known as silver, being black and white striped; the breast is slightly tinged with salmon-colour. The next class is a larger one—the grays; these may be of any colour, provided they are not brown: ash, cobweb with dark hackle, semi-white with dark spots, light gray, pencilled with darker shades of the same colour. With all these, the most desirable match for a cock is one with light hackle and saddle, dark breast and tail; I advisedly say dark in preference to black, because I think servile adherence to any given colour too often necessitates the sacrifice of more valuable qualities. I look on a fine Dorking cock with no less admiration if his breast is speckled, and his tail composed of a mixture of black and white feathers; and such a bird is a fit and proper mate for any gray hens. But the gray must not be confounded with the speckle: these have a brown ground with white spots. One of the best judges I know of a Dorking fowl properly describes them as brown hens covered with flakes of snow. These speckled hens are of two distinct colours: the first is known as Sir John Cathcart's colour; the pullets are of a rich chocolate, splashed or spotted with white; the cocks are either black-breasted reds without mixture, or spotted like the hens on the breast and partially on the body: it is no objection if

COLOURED DORKING.

the tail is partly coloured. Another speckle is of a grayish-brown spotted with white: these hens should have a cock with dark hackle and saddle, and the wings and back should show some red or chestnut feathers: these last are not essential, but *a light cock* will not match *speckled hens*. Next we have brown hens: these should have a black-breasted red cock, but a speckled one will pass muster."

These birds took their name from the town of Dorking, in Surrey; they are essentially an English fowl, not being known, as far as we are aware, in any other part of the world. There are two, if not three, very distinct breeds of Dorkings. One is pure white, with a broad double, or, as it is termed, rose comb, and five distinct toes on both feet. This breed is not, however, in such great request as the Coloured Dorking.

In this latter breed, the plumage varies very much, some are speckled; others, known as the Cuckoo Dorkings, have their feathers transversely barred like those on the breast and under side of the Cuckoo; and a third set have very nearly the markings of a Duckwing game. As a good horse can hardly be of a bad colour, so the same remark holds true of a good Dorking. It may be asked, then, what are the characteristics of a good Dorking?

Firstly, large size: as Dorkings are, above all, table fowls, size is absolutely requisite to constitute preeminence, eight to ten pounds each for the cocks, and six to eight pounds for the hens, are averages they must be kept to if success in Dorking breeding is looked for. The form is almost as essential as the size; a Dorking, whether cock or hen, must be compact in the body, with short legs and shanks. The very qualities that add grace and gallant bearing to the Spanish and Game, render the Dorking unfit for table purposes; and, therefore, a short, stout limb is aimed at, and regarded as perfection in this breed. The shanks, or scaly part of the leg, must be white, the claims of the fancier and of the cook imperatively demanding a colourless leg in this breed; the fancier demands it because such is the

standard of excellence universally received; and the cook because a boiled fowl with black legs does not look sightly on the dinner-table.

The toes, in the Dorking, must be five in number. Fashion, which in poultry, as in everything else, is tyrannous and despotic, will accept no fowl as a true Dorking that has only four toes; not that there is any real utility in this extra toe, which can only be regarded as a sort of monstrosity; but because birds will not sell as Dorkings that have not got them. Everybody who hatches a four-toed bird kills it, and only breeds from the five-toed cocks and hens. The combs of Dorkings are of two kinds, that known as the double or rose comb, is characteristic of some breeds; whilst others have an upright single comb, regularly serrated or toothed, like that shown in the Dorking cock in the engraving on page 29.

Having spoken of their characteristics, it now remains to say something respecting the properties of the Dorkings as useful fowls. It has been said of them that their quality surpasses their charms; but we must confess that no birds to our mind look more in keeping with a farm-yard or homestead, than a good collection of Dorkings, the cocks heavy, broad-chested, weighty birds, the hens ponderous and sedate in their movements, looking like the grave dowagers of the poultry yard. As layers, Dorking hens are surpassed by many other breeds, especially by those that do not sit; but as mothers, for large chickens, none can excel them. From their weight they are not adapted to become foster mothers and hatch and rear the eggs of the lighter kinds; but for sitting on the eggs of either Spanish or Cochin, or for rearing their own chickens, they are not to be surpassed.

Unfortunately, they are not so hardy as many other breeds; on cold clay soils they are reared with much more difficulty than either Cochin or game; this is a great drawback to their utility in such situations. But on chalky or gravelly soil, where the ground dries in a short time after every shower, they do well, and there are no birds that pay better. Good Dorkings are always in request for stock purposes, and those that are killed for the table always command the highest price in the market. Their white skin and fat white legs, and plump full breasts, rendering them the best and most valued of all table poultry.

HAMBURGHS.

In contrast to the Dorking, I will now speak of the Spangled Hamburgh, or Pheasant Fowl, as it is very commonly termed in Yorkshire and Lancashire, where the breed exists in the greatest purity, and in the largest numbers. These birds, which are also termed Moonies, are the most beautifully marked of any variety of domestic poultry. In a well-spangled hen, every feather of the body and tail is tipped with a large black moon or spangle, hence the name Moony or Spangle. The tail feathers should also be regularly spangled or mooned in the same manner, those of the neck being streaked with black. Across the wing should be two rows of spangles forming a couple of bars.

The ground colour of the feathers varies in the two varieties. In what are called Gold-Spangled Hamburghs, the ground is of a rich deep bay; but in the Silver Spangles it is of a pure white colour.

The chief points of excellence to be aimed at in this breed are the pureness of the ground colour, and the large size and distinctness of the black moons at the tips of the feathers. In addition to these points, there are others which are regarded as indispensable in the breed. One is, that the comb should be a neat double comb, covered evenly with small pointed sprigs, and ending in a spike behind. The legs must be blue, and the toes only four in number. These fowls possess certain qualities that render them most valuable in a profitable point of view. Not one hen in five hundred ever shows the least inclination to sit upon or hatch her eggs; so that the chicken must be reared by other

3

hens that retain their maternal instinct. This peculiarity must not, however, be regarded as a drawback to the value of the Hamburghs in an economical point of view; it is, in fact, their greatest recommendation: for, instead of being broody and wishing to sit, they go on, if well fed, laying all the year round, with the exception of the time they are moulting during the autumn.

Every one of these hens can be depended on for laying, on an average, 200 eggs in the year. And I should have no objection to staking a heavy wager that five hens of this breed would, barring accidents and illness, produce over 1000 eggs annually. In the true sense of the word, they are, in the second and third years of their lives, everlasting layers; after that age, however, they fall off somewhat in this respect.

Their eggs are a little below the average size, as might be expected, when it is remembered that the birds themselves are smaller than the Dorking or the Spanish breed.

Another great recommendation of Spangled Hamburghs is, that they are good foragers: they roam much, and find a great portion of their own food. Their powers of flight are very great; in fact, they can fly almost, if not quite, as well as pheasants, hence they are rather difficult to keep within bounds; but, in situations where they can roam about, I do not know any variety of fowl that can be kept to greater advantage. They are the most profitable of egg-producers; and their beauty renders them as attractive in an ornamental point of view as they are useful from economical considerations.

Let such of my readers as live in the south of England, not attempt to purchase Spangled Hamburghs in their own locality; it is in the northern counties only that they are to be obtained in full perfection and purity of breed.

An amateur breeder of fowls says, " The Spangled birds are not obtained from Holland, but are bred in Lancashire and Yorkshire, of which counties I believe them to be natives, though they are said also to be common in Russia and Northern Europe. The Spangled Hamburghs, or Pheasant Fowls, as the North-country breeders call them, are, in my judgment, the best and most regular layers I can recommend; but in this respect the gold and silver varieties somewhat differ. I have generally found that the pullets of the former variety commence laying at about six months old, and, if the season is moderately warm, they continue to lay about nine eggs a fortnight, until their moulting-time the following year—I should say, that on an average, they lay about 200 eggs per annum. They are everlasting layers, in the strictest sense of the word, never sitting, and recommencing their labours of production about two months from the commencement of their moult. Their eggs are of a fair size, of a very light pinky brown colour, and excellent flavour. Indeed, in the latter quality the eggs of the Hamburgh fowls generally are not to be surpassed.

"It is the birds of silver variety, however, which I regard and recommend as perfect miracles of egg-producing constancy. They commence laying, if in good health and with a *good run* (an essential to the well-doing of both the varieties), at *five* months old, and generally lay at least six days out of the seven, until the moulting season arrives—in all probability some 250 eggs. They very quickly get their new plumage —and in six weeks recommence their labours with the same praiseworthy diligence, until another season passed warns them that moulting-time is again at hand. After the second year I do not consider it advisable to keep them for laying purposes, although I think the best chickens are bred from them after that period with a young yearling cock.

"Like their golden relations, they never sit, and rarely evince the slightest desire to undertake the task of incubation. I feel quite confident that no fowl produces so much *egg stuff* with so *small an amount of food*. Give them a good run, a clean, dry, warm house at night, and one quarter of the food you bestow upon

Cochins, and you will have no further trouble with them. They feather early and quickly, and may safely be hatched early in April.

"I must not, however, omit to state one drawback which there is to the keeping my spangled pets—they fly like pheasants, and know not bounds. They are great enemies to flowers, fruit, vegetables, indeed, anything they can lay hold of; and although capable of being made as tame as any other fowls, in their instincts they seem almost more like game than domesticated poultry. However, as a balance to this, there is no fowl so capable of taking care of itself, of finding its own food, of avoiding danger, and of repaying its owner handsomely for the slight care it demands at his or her hands. Indeed, I cannot recommend to a beginner in poultry-keeping a more beautiful and interesting, or a more profitable selection.

"There is much difference of opinion about the desired points of beauty in these birds. For the exact requirements in the North-country shows I must refer my readers to the rules of the Yorkshire societies, and I will therefore confine myself to a brief and general description of what I consider requisite for perfection in these birds. And firstly as to the golden variety; although, with the exception of a few observations which I shall make about the cocks, the same points are almost requisite in both varieties.

" In the cocks, the comb should be flat, rose, stretching far back on the head, and ending in a pike—at least an inch and a quarter in width, and as square in shape as possible; the ear lobe white; the neck hackle, in the golden variety, of which I am now speaking, black fringled with gold; the back, breast, and legs, regularly spangled, and the larger and brighter green black the spangles the better; the saddle feathers small and spangled; the tail long, full, and of a brilliant green black; the legs light grey blue; toe-nails white. The same description applies to the hens, which should have a flat rose comb, not lopping, but upright; the ground colour of the plumage should be a rich red gold or burnt sienna colour. One great point of beauty also, both in the cocks and hens, is, that the wings should be regularly laced, as in the spangled Polands. The great difficulty in breeding the cocks is the tendency they have to come with black breasts and red backs—and for show such birds are valueless, although, it is said, more likely to throw good pullets than the spangled breasted birds, which are sometimes termed hen-feathered. The *silver* spangled cock should not be hen-feathered, the hackle, and saddle feathers should be white, the latter very long, the tail spangled black and white, the breast regularly spangled up to the throat, and in colour the clearest white for the ground, and the brightest green black for the spangles, is requisite. The lacing of the wing in this variety is quite a *sine quâ non*, both in the cocks and hens; and in the latter the tail should be clear white, with three or four large circular spangles upon it, but no other dark markings whatever. The neck, back, breast, rump, and legs should be regularly spangled, and there should be a total absence of patchiness in the markings. In both varieties great distinctness of colour is requisite, and from the delicacy of the plumage the slightest approach to breeding *in and in* is sure to make the produce utterly valueless. In conclusion, the carriage of the cocks should be lofty and upright, with the breast thrown forward like the Polands; the weight of the male birds from five pounds to six pounds, of the hens from four pounds to five pounds, or a little more."

Pencilled Hamburghs.—These are found in two colours, gold and silver; each, however, with the body feathers distinctly marked, or pencilled in cross-bars. They are handsome, graceful birds, good layers, but very bad sitters. Though the best and largest kinds are now bred in this country, great numbers are annually imported from Holland.

POLAND FOWLS.

There are several varieties of these handsome fowls. They are good layers but they will not sit. In this

respect they are worse than the Spanish and Hamburgh. All the Polish fowls are distinguished by a
large top-knot (which, in the hens, forms a dense round
turf) and a small semi-circular comb. The Spangled
Polands are likewise distinguished by a beard. They

are excellent for the table, as they grow plump and eat
tender; but their small size rather detracts from their
value as fowls for market. Except on sandy, chalky,
and other very dry soils, Polands can hardly be said to
be profitable to keep or breed.

BANTAMS.

No poultry fowl exists in so many varieties as the
Bantam; but whether known as Black, White, Gold-
laced, Silver-laced, Game, Booted, or what not, they
have all certain characteristics in common—diminutive
size, grace of outline, and beauty of plumage. Bantams
can hardly be called "profitable," though they are good
layers and sitters. Indeed, they are generally kept
rather for ornament than service. "Feather-legged
Bantams," says Mr. Bailey, "may be of any colour;
the old-fashioned birds are very small, falcon-hocked,
and feathered with long quill feathers to the extremity
of the toe. Many of them were bearded. They are
now very scarce; indeed, till exhibitions brought them
again into notice, these beautiful specimens of their
tribe were all neglected and fast passing away. Nothing

but the Sebright was cultivated; but now we bid fair
to revive the pets of our ancestors in all their beauty."

Game Bantams are in every respect miniature repe-
titions of the old English Game Cock, with abundance of
pertness, closeness of feather, strut, brilliancy of colour,
and undoubted pluck.   Bantams are always favourites

with the ladies, and at exhibitions are sure to attract
attention.

LA FLÊCHE.

This is described by Miss Watts as the best of
the French fowls. " It is," she says, " a handsome, upstanding, hardy bird, easily reared, of quick
growth, and a layer of large eggs. The colour of the

fowl is jet black, with a very rich metallic lustre; the ear-lobe large and quite white, the face unusually free from feathers, and of a bright red. In good specimens the comb never varies in either sex: it is in the shape of a pair of straight horns. The nostrils are large and elevated, the scales on the legs seem hard and firm, and are of a bright lead colour. These birds have more size and style about them than the Crêve Cœurs, and they are better adapted to our climate. The cock birds stand high on the leg, but without being leggy, as the breasts are full and the bodies well hung. The hens have large, long bodies, thin legs, and long necks. They are found in the north of France, but they are not by any means plentiful there, as the French, except a few amateurs, do not keep breeds of fowls distinct, consequently, even in their own district, they are not easily obtained, and sell for high prices."

CHAPTER III.

PROFITABLE POULTRY.

If you want to produce a large number of eggs, the Hamburghs are the best where your space is large, and Cochins and Spanish where room is restricted. Hamburghs are good winter layers, but Cochins are also very productive.

"Cochin chickens," says Miss Watts, "are backward in fledging, and chickens bred from immature fowls are the worst in this particular. Although backward in fledging, however, they early reach maturity; and we have had pullets laying at fourteen weeks old, and wanting to sit under six months from the time of being hatched. Cochin breeders, of course, try to prevent such precocity, as it interferes with size, at any rate at an early age. When the young birds show an inclination to develop too early, it is advisable to avoid giving meat and all forcing diet. The Cochin hen's propensity to become broody very often is a great inconvenience to those who keep them, since many hens will take to the nest several times in one season. A little care will obviate the evil; but of course it interferes with the supply of eggs."

Fowls are distinguished by many peculiarities. Some are disposed to lay eggs at all times of the year, without at any time showing an inclination to sit upon them, others lay at particular seasons, while others, again, seem to think that when they have laid a dozen or fifteen eggs they must sit upon them and hatch them right away. In order that there may be no mistake, I give the following. :—

Fowls that lay freely and sit readily.—1. Bantams of all kinds; 2. Game Fowl of every variety; 3. Dorkings, in which term are included the Speckled, the Surrey, the Old Kent, the Cuckoo, and the Coloured; 4. Cochin-Chinas; 5. Malay; 6. Dark-crested Fowl.

Fowls that lay well but will rarely sit.—1. Spanish of all kinds; 2. Hamburghs; 3. Polands.

In making a profit of poultry, care must be taken that you select the right sorts. Keep partridge-coloured Cochin China and speckled Dorking pullets in equal numbers, none older than a year, with one Dorking cock to each half-dozen pullets. By this plan you will have a good supply of eggs at all seasons, and all the chickens will be excellent for the table.

If you decide on *rearing chickens as well as producing eggs*, then you must have hens that will both lay and sit readily. As actual experience is of more value than mere theory, I give the results of experiments made by a well-known amateur and contributor to the " Cottage Gardener :"—

" I have long kept hens for the purposes of profit only, and the point to which I would call attention is, the very small profit balance for the large number of ' more than one thousand chickens annually hatched,' which profit would be reduced to a certain loss had the expenses of exhibiting been placed on the debit side.

" In the county in which I resided (Shropshire), on my first essay in poultry-keeping, eggs were worth 1*s.* only per score in the laying season, and fat fowls were considered dear at 4*s.* the couple, the more usual prices being from 2*s.* 6*d.* to 3*s.* I have purchased fat young ducks at 2*s.* 6*d.* the couple, when, as the local phrase hath it, the vendor had ' overstood the market.'

" I had kept hens with profit, even at the prices given above, when I removed into Hertfordshire, and there became acquainted with the system of poultry-keeping on a large scale, and in which the balance is on the right side of the account, to the tune of some—not tens, nor even hundreds, but thousand of pounds in the aggregate.

" This insight decided my course. I commenced at once, though on a very moderate scale; and I will give the results I attained.

" My accounts begin but imperfectly; but when fairly at work, a daily journal was kept—not a chicken nor an egg being disposed of without an entry of the price obtained, and when for home consumption entered at cost price. On the other hand, all grain, meal, bran, and the several et ceteras for poultry-feeding, were duly placed on the debit side; and at the year's end, a moderate charge was made for management, rent, and interest, thus putting to the proof whether or not poultry-keeping is profitable.

"I can safely aver it is, and that to a great extent; the fact being established, profit is only a matter of degree. The want of capital alone prevents me turning my knowledge and practice to good account.

"I remember a writer stating that 'a hen was as profitable as a sheep.' I agree with this assertion.

"My first attempt at poultry-keeping on system was commenced with hens of every and of no breed. I got them as I could, from the common barndoor fowl to the stately Spanish and aristocratic Game. But even this had its advantages, enabling me to form a just estimate of their peculiar good qualities, and to discard the comparatively worthless. For all purposes, however, I prefer the Dorking, and the speckled of that breed for choice, whether for the table or for their eggs. With me they answered best, and were in more general demand by the poultry dealers.

"Here are the results of my poultry-keeping for profit.

"The following account is drawn by striking the average of three years for 100 hens, having a run of about two acres of grass land, and about a quarter of an acre of yard :—

Dr. EXPENDITURE.	£ s. d.	Cr. RECEIPTS.	£ s. d.
To food	31 16 0	By return from 100 hens, at 18s. 9d.	
To rent, management, loss, and interest .	16 12 0	a head	93 15 0
By profit—Balance .	45 7 0		
	£93 15 0		£93 15 0

Or about 90 per cent.

"Now, supposing the quantity of stock kept to reach the number of 500 hens, if the poultry-keeper's wife charged her own services at £52 a-year, and those of a strong active girl at £30, including her maintenance— £82 per annum, it will be seen how handsome a return would even then be derived from this branch of rural economy.

"And now for an analysis of the items of the above account. I will premise that the above profits can readily be exceeded, if fattening fowls were the chief aim. For instance: if my reader will refer to the Cr. side, he will find that I give the return of each hen at 18s. 9d. Thus, a hen will lay on an average

120 eggs at 1d.	10s.	0d.
Besides hatching a brood, of which she will rear, on an average, 7 chickens, at 1s. 3d.	8	9
	18s.	9d.

"I found the expense of rearing chickens up to the age of from ten to twelve weeks did not much exceed 1d. per head per week, and having a good grass run. Hence, if a couple of chickens cost 1s. 8d. to rear for sale, and then brought 2s. 6d., the profit would be 50 per cent.; but if they were kept until they were five months old, costing 2s., they were then worth 4s. 6d. or 5s. each, thus giving the extraordinary profit of 125 or 150 per cent.

"To obtain these prices, however, it is but right to say, that the young poultry *must* be ready for market when game is out of season, and just at Christmas; for though game comes in in August, it is not until the partridge falls that the poultry-keeper finds the demand lessen and prices drop.

"Much has been said and written relative to the soil on which hens and their chickens best thrive. There can be no question that sand or gravel is to be preferred; but let none despair should their lot be cast on a stiff clay, for it was on such that the results given were obtained.

"And now for the life of a chicken from the nest to the salesman. This I will endeavour to exemplify by a few simple rules, which will require the exercise of common sense only to bring matters to a successful issue.

"*Keeping of Eggs for Sitting.*—Eggs intended to be used for sitting should never be laid on their sides, but retained in an upright position, with the narrow end downwards. This is readily managed by putting a few inches of moss into a shallow box, and placing the eggs therein.

"*Sitting the Hens.*—In spring and summer put the 'magic number,' thirteen eggs, under the hens: but in autumn and winter do not exceed nine or ten; and care must be taken that the eggs are all of one day's laying, if possible. More depends upon attention to this than may at first sight appear. It is well to sit more than one hen on the same day, should you be so fortunate as to have more than one hen broody. This simplifies after-management, by making one hen nurse two hatches; and allows the other to recover strength and come into laying again sooner. If possible, sit on the ground; but should the hen have chosen her nest do not disturb her, unless the situation be manifestly disadvantageous, and place a large turf under her.

"*Hatching Time.*—If attention was given at sitting time to use none but eggs of an equal age, the chicks will, as a rule, break the shell within a few hours of each other. New-laid eggs will be hatched under the twenty-one days; fresh eggs (those laid three days or a week before sitting), will take the entire time; and stale (though not unprofitable eggs), I have known take from twenty-two to twenty-four days. Chicks from the latter are generally not so lively, and do scarcely so well; but I have rarely noticed any difference between those from new-laid and those from fresh eggs, as to their after-thriving, each coming as early to profit as the other. It is a most reprehensible practice to remove the chickens from the nest as they are hatched;

it irritates the parent bird, and I think it is positively essential to the well-being of the young ones to be left with the hen. I cannot lay too great stress on this point, for it is the fruitful source of disappointment and loss. When all are free from the shell, entice the hen off the nest by throwing down some food, and then remove the shells. Do not afterwards disturb her for twelve hours or so. She knows when her young are strong enough to move about, so leave this to her.

"*After-Management.*—When the hen comes off of her own accord, you may know all is right with the chicks. Occasionally place the hen under a coop, and allow the chicks but a limited run for the first fortnight, especially guarding them from contact with wet grass— they cannot, in fact, be kept too dry. Thus care should be taken that the water-pans are shallow. Many things are recommended as the best food for young chicks, but I never found *anything answer so well as crumbs of stale home-made bread;* and as to the different nostrums propounded, I notice them only to condemn them *in toto*. The hen should be well fed on grain, meal, and steamed potatoes, and grass and leaves from garden vegetables daily. It is a good rule to remove the coop a few feet every day or two, so that the hen may have a fresh and dry soil, and she should have a moderate quantity of sand or light mould placed under her coop, in which to bathe. In a week or so give the hen her liberty, feed her chickens with her, and they will thrive right well and merrily. I found, however, that those chicks did best where the hen, after having her liberty during the day, at night was put under a coop; she then nestled her young instead of flying on to the perch.

"*Management of Chickens when Discarded by the Hen.* —In about eight or nine weeks, according to the season of the year, the hen will forsake her brood. Now part the stronger chickens from the weaker, and hasten on by generous food for sale. Much might be written on the all-important point of feeding; but I shall give that course which answered well with me. I fed four times a-day—oftener if I saw occasion, or the weather demanded it. On this point no rule can be laid down, it must be left to the judgment.

"1st meal.—Meat scraps chopped, and dry barley.

"2nd ditto.—Steamed potatoes, mixed with steeped oats, rice, or crushed Indian corn or meal.

"3rd ditto.—Barley, tail wheat, and tallow greaves.

"4th ditto.—Dry grain.

"And twice a week mashed bran.

"I took care that on no two consecutive days did I feed exactly alike, for every animal thrives on variation of food. Besides the stated feeding times, all the remnants from the table and the kitchen, such as crumbs, meat, bones, and vegetables, were thrown down to them. In the winter and early spring months bullock's liver, and other cheap animal offal, should be boiled for both hens and chickens; put the broth therefrom, when cool, into their drinking-pans, and chop up the meat, mixing it with their grain, or giving it alone.

"'And is this all?' my uninitiated reader may ask. Yea, truly, all the whole secret.

"I shall now suppose my chickens three months old.

"'Well, my friend,' I say to the poultry dealer who calls, 'what will you give me for this lot?'

"'Well, chickens is down, they ain't worth ne'er so much as they was last week.'

"'Ah, is that so? Now, though you are called a higgler, I don't like haggling; so, at a word, what is your offer?'

"'Master, I can't be buyer *and* seller too.'

"'Well, my price is 3*s.* the couple for the smaller chickens, and 3*s.* 6*d.* for the larger.'

"'Then I shan't get no profit by 'em.'

"'They are worth it; and I do not feel disposed to take less.'

"'Then it's no deal.'

"And off goes the higgler. But wait a wee. He

well knows they *are* worth the money, and in half an hour or so returns, pays you the sum asked with the air of a man who has done you, ties the chickens in couples, places them in his basket, and departs.

"And now, reader, what has been my profit?

"Over 60 per cent. assuredly; and if these said chicks had been less than pigeons early in March, I could have had 2s. 6d. *each*, and my profit would then have considerably exceeded 100 per cent.

"'And not bad interest either,' say you.

"To those who may feel inclined to try their hands at poultry-keeping I would say, 'Take care of your old birds.' By these I do not mean hens of some three or four years, but those which may be falling off in productiveness, or that may have been disabled by accident but not vitally injured; for from these will be obtained the larger profits of their undertaking.

"Put such at once up to feed, placing them in pens, or in any confined corners where they can be kept warm and dry, and feed liberally; and if the 'cramming system' be resorted to, they will be fit to send to market as capon. A fowl of some eighteen or twenty months old, healthy, but worth little to sell—say 1s. 6d., may, by extra feeding and good management, quickly be made worth 5s. or 6s.

"It is unnecessary to advert to the description of bird held to make the best capon; but, whichever it may be, breed and manage as now stated.

"Beat equal portions of wheat and barley-meal, and occasionally Indian corn-meal, into a stiff paste with steamed potatoes. When the bird has eaten to repletion and leaves its trough, take it firmly but gently under the left arm, with the left hand open the beak, and with the right place divers and sundry boluses of the same food at the root of the tongue, and the bird will continue to feed for some time longer. Use judgment, and you will soon know when to stay. Now endeavour to induce sleep by placing the head under the wing; and, giving the bird a few gentle waves or rocking motion in the air, place it on the perch, and darken the pen by any convenient means (nothing better than an old sack). This course of feeding must be resorted to often during the day, and the fowl must be kept well supplied with drink, and this should, if possible, be milk. Broth will do, but milk is to be preferred, both for fatting and for the colour of the flesh.

"Should this plan be followed out on birds of from five to nine months old they will fatten more quickly, but the price obtained will not be much in advance of that for the older birds."

CHAPTER IV.

BREEDING.

HAVING shown that in order to make fowls profitable, you should attend—1, to the selection of the proper kinds; 2, to the regular supply of food and water; and 3, to the comfortable housing and care of your stock—it remains but to briefly discuss the subject of breeding and diseases.

On the first topic, an amateur hen-wife says:—"The most usual time in which hens manifest a desire to incubate extends from March to May or June, and at this season chickens may be reared without any extra precautions. The hens selected should be of medium size; not too old, in good plumage, and with short legs. The number of eggs allotted to each hen may vary from nine to fourteen; never more. It is a good plan, as I have already remarked, to set two hens on the same day, and when the broods come forth, to give the maternal charge of both to one of the hens. Some persons remove the other to a fresh set of eggs, which, if she be a steady sitter, she will hatch. This, however, must be deemed a cruelty; some hens would sit until they became so feeble and emaciated as to be restored with difficulty. But to sit twice is a tax on the system; and no one but a person dead to feelings of consideration for the lower animals would permit a hen, however constant to her task, to sit three or four times.

" For the nest of the sitter warmth and moisture are important things; if it be moist and warm so much the better, but cold moisture is fatal to the hopes of the hatching. If the soil is warm let the hens choose their own nests, and sit upon the ground; but if it is cold, give them good thick warm nests of well-rubbed straw, dried heath, or fern. The hen should be encouraged to leave her nest every morning, and should have a supply of food and water, with gravel and dust to pick amongst, and to roll in if she choose. The person who has charge of the sitters should know when the hens leave their nests, and see that each one gets plenty of food and water without loss of time; for, poor things! this is the only meal of creatures in the habit of eating every hour in the day, and they want it. Interference beyond this needful attention cannot be too much condemned.

"When hens want to sit, and it is not wished that they should do so, change of scene is the best cure. Remove them from the hen-run to some spot quite away from it, on grass if convenient, and in a very few days the fancy will be forgotten, and in due time they will recommence laying.

"In selecting eggs for hatching choose the newest; care should be taken that they are not above a fortnight or three weeks old; and if they are under a week old so much the better. Large rounded eggs, with double yolks, are apt to do no good, or to produce monstrosities. If the eggs are all of the same age to a day, the better.

"Let us now suppose that the chick has opened the door of its egg. It is free; while yet on the threshold of the egg, having already drawn its head from under its wing, and directed it forwards, the neck trembling beneath the weight which it has now for the first time to sustain. With its neck stretched forwards, and unable to raise itself upon its legs, it rests for a few minutes till its strength is recruited; the fresh air revives it, it raises itself up, it lifts its head, it turns its neck from side to side, and begins to feel its innate powers. Its downy plumage, the precursor of feathers, being wet with the fluid of the egg, lies close to the skin, in stripes down the body and on the wings; besides, it has not yet become fairly freed from the

4—2

sheath in which every plumelet is inclosed. As it dries, every tuft expands or opens like a feathery flower; the little membranous sheaths split and fall off; and the chick rises in its nest, and nestles into the mother's plumage, clothed with a downy garment of exquisite delicacy.

" Occasionally, perhaps, among wild birds, there occur instances in which chicks perish in the egg, unable to extricate themselves from the shell and membranes. We say perhaps; but if our own experience does not deceive us, such instances not unfrequently occur; the chick is dried or glued to its shell, and unless assistance be given, will infallibly perish. In the case of the wild bird, assistance is out of the question; but in her great course Nature designs the strong alone to live and perpetuate the species. If this accident occurs among wild birds, much more frequently, as might be expected, does it occur among our domesticated stocks. It is said the later eggs of a hen are more liable to this casualty than those laid at the commencement of the season, but we have never found this to be the case, provided the weather be favourable.

"The more completely the hen and hatching brood are left to themselves and to Nature the better. If assistance seems necessary, be very cautious not to give it too soon, for in that case the chicken is almost *sure* to die. Go to work cautiously, tenderly, and slowly, and not until you have good reasons to believe the chick is unable to extricate itself."

For the first day the chicks require neither food nor water; the old plan of cramming peppercorns and so on down the throats of the little things is both cruel and absurd. On and after the second day feed them as already directed on page 15, giving them a little chopped onion occasionally, or green onion-tops, to lessen their chance of croup. Some hens do not need to be cooped, but may be allowed to wander with their chicks immediately, when they begin to scratch for worms and insects, their natural food. A large chicken-coop, for feeding chickens under, without the hen, is a very useful addition to the fowl-yard. Above all, let the little ones have plenty of fresh air, wholesome food, clean grass and clean water.

With regard to the age of parents, I believe that it "is not so desirable to breed from hens in their first as in their second or third years. The chickens of first-year fowls are more leggy, smaller, and less hardy and vigorous than those produced by more mature parents. When young birds are employed, it is desirable to mate pullets with cocks two or three years old, and cockerels with old hens. Some persons even carry their objection so far, as not to allow young birds to hatch the eggs of older birds, being under the impression they do not sit with sufficient steadiness. This is certainly not true as regards Dorkings and Cochins. To insure healthy and large-sized chickens, it is absolutely necessary that there should be no relationship between the parents. Breeding 'in and in,' as it is termed, produces diseased and weakly offspring, hence it is indispensable that there should be an introduction of fresh male birds every two or three years. In farm-yards where there are large numbers of poultry, it will be found by far the most desirable plan to keep separately a cock with from four to six of the best hens, and to hatch their eggs alone. By this means the chickens are all certain of coming from the best birds, and a much smaller number of cocks may be kept with the main stock of hens than would otherwise be desirable. The practice of allowing the hens to run with several cocks is calculated to deteriorate the breed materially; should therefore a larger number of eggs be required for hatching than furnished by a cock and four or six hens, another set should be separated."

ARTIFICIAL HATCHING.

The plan of hatching eggs without a hen has been practised by the Egyptians from a very early period. About one hundred and twenty years ago, the celebrated naturalist, M. de Reaumur, performed a number of experiments, and repeated all the processes of the Egyptians. He built large ovens, and hatched great numbers of young chickens; but as the colder climate of France is not so favourable to the rearing of the young birds as that of Egypt, he did not succeed so well as to prove that the method was superior in economy to that of hatching by hens. All the experiments he performed, and the plans he pursued, are described in a large work which he published, which was beautifully illustrated with copper-plates, showing the ovens, the growth of the chick within the shell, and the whole of the apparatus employed.

In our own country there was an exhibition of an egg-hatching machine in Pall Mall. It was called the Eccaleobion, and when I was a boy it attracted a great deal of attention. Some time after this, a Mr. Cantelo patented a new machine for hatching. He took a poultry farm in the country, and opened an exhibition at Saville House, Leicester Square, and hatched cocks and hens in the room in which the Queen's grandfather, George the Third, was born; for George the Second's son, who was then Frederick, Prince of Wales, lived at Saville Palace. But the steam-hatching scheme collapsed, without making its proprietor's fortune.

Since that time, Mr. Minasi invented a new machine, and one of another kind has been employed in hatching out the eggs of valuable foreign birds that have been laid in the Zoological Gardens.

When young I wanted to hatch some chickens to study the mode in which they grew in the shell, as I was living in London, attending lectures, and walking the hospitals, as it is called. I could not get my chickens hatched under hens, so I set my wits to work to make an incubator to hatch them in my bedroom. As I had not more money than I knew what to do with, I was obliged to be very economical, and go to work the cheapest way. So I went to a second-hand tool shop, and bought an old glue-pot for eighteenpence. My bedroom was lighted with a gas-burner; consequently, all that I had to do for heating my incubator was to hang it over the gas at such a distance that it could be regulated to the proper temperature.

The outer vessel was filled with water, or so far filled that the water came nearly up to the top when the inner vessel was pressed down. A little fine sand was placed at the bottom of the inner vessel; on this the eggs were placed, and covered over with a few folds of soft flannel to prevent the heat escaping.

In this way I hatched and half hatched many chickens, and my microscope was always at work, finding out how the heart grew and acted, and how the different organs of the body were developed or formed one after the other.

I soon found, however, that my glue-pot was not altogether the best thing that I could use, for a good many of the chickens died before the eggs had been many days in the heat. For a long time I could not think of the cause, but at last it struck me that the impure and foul air arising from the burning of the gas would find its way over the top into the inner vessel, and injuriously affect the eggs. So I made a contrivance for carrying away the foul air, or, as our professor of chemistry learnedly called it, "the vitiated and impure products of combustion." This contrivance was made of stout paper, which surrounded the glue-pot, and there was a tube or chimney to take away the air; it worked very well for some days, but got rather dingy and brown. One evening, on going home after the lecture, I found it had caught fire, burnt the paper and paint of the room, and nearly set the house on fire, so I determined to have nothing more to do with the glue-pot; but contrived the following improved machine, which worked very well.

The apparatus was made of tin. First there was an outer case open both at top and below, it was like a four-sided box without a lid or a bottom. At one end of this was a round hole, into which a pipe was soldered; this pipe served as a chimney to carry off the gas and smoke from the lamp, which was placed at the other end, where there was an opening to admit air to the flame, and a door so that the lamp could be taken out when it was necessary to trim it and replenish it with oil.

After a time I found that it was desirable to have a window in the door, so that the state of the flame could be seen without the trouble of opening the door: consequently I cut a hole in the door, and put in a piece of glass.

At the top of this tin case there was a deep hollow tray, the exact size of the box, into which it was closely fitted: this tray was prevented from going down too deeply into the box by a flange, or rim, at its upper edge, which rested on the edge of the box.

When the tray was filled with warm water, and the lamp lighted, it could be kept at any desired temperature by raising or lowering the flame. In my young days there were no paraffin lamps, so I was obliged to use oil, which was much more expensive. The temperature that the water should be kept at is about 106 degrees on the common thermometer used in England.

Inside this water tray was placed a second one, which dropped into it just in the same manner as it dropped into the box: this tray, like all the other parts, was made of tin. In the bottom was placed an inch depth of clean white silver sand, on this the eggs were laid, and then over the top a number of folds of soft flannel laid lightly on, and not pressed down on the eggs, a common thermometer was laid in the sand, and the flame so regulated that the heat should never rise above 104 degrees, as a very few degrees higher will kill all the chickens in the eggs.

No other particular direction is necessary, except that the eggs should be turned every day.

At the end of a week, after the first batch of eggs is put in, you may examine them. To do this, cut an oval hole in a board, or a piece of a book-cover will do:

let this hole be of such a size that an egg can be held against it without going through. If this board is placed on its edge, with a candle on one side, and you hold the egg to be examined at the other, you will see if the egg is bad or good. If after being in the incubator or under a hen for a week, it is clear and transparent as it was at first, you may remove it at once, as it will never produce a chicken; but if, on the other hand, it is quite dark, or opaque, except a clear space at the large end, then there is a growing chicken in the inside.

Of course you will at once take all your clear eggs out of the incubator, and supply their places with fresh ones, if you want more chickens; and recollect that the clear eggs that you remove, though not very good food for your own breakfast-table, answer very well for the breakfast of the young chicks that have been already hatched. For this purpose they should be boiled hard and mixed with the bread-crumb and oatmeal that constitutes their first dietary. Of course you will expect me to tell you how long the eggs will be in hatching out. That, of course, depends on the birds that have laid them. Fowls' eggs hatch out on that day three weeks that the eggs are placed in the incubator; ducks' eggs take a few days longer, depending very much on the season of the year and the temperature of the hot sand. If you should put an ostrich's egg in your apparatus, you will have to wait fifty-eight days before a young ostrich makes its appearance, and that is the longest time that the egg of any bird takes to hatch.

I have now to direct attention to the manner in which the chickens are to be reared after they have been hatched. The rearing of the young chickens cannot, in our cold climate, be accomplished with so great an amount of success as it can in Egypt, where hatching ovens, or *mammals*, as they are called, have existed from very remote periods.

In this country the best mother is a hen who has but

a small brood of her own, and by far the most profitable mode of using an incubator, is to place a second sitting of eggs in it, on the same day that a hen is sat. It rarely, if ever, happens, that the number of chickens hatched out by the hen and the incubator combined will be more than the hen can cover and attend to, and in this way a large instead of small brood of chickens may be obtained.

Some hens will always take to a brood of chickens at any time. We once had a Cochin that possessed this peculiarity. We could put her down on the lawn in front of our house, place a dozen eggs before her, when she would pull them under her with her beak, and would sit as complacently upon them as she could have done in the most cosy hen-house. In the same manner she would receive strange chickens and adopt them as her own. But such hens are very rare, and therefore, in order to rear the chickens hatched by the incubator, *an artificial mother* must be made.

The principle on which these are generally constructed, is that of a metallic vessel of hot water standing on very short feet. The under side of this should be covered with a layer of blanket or wool, and around the sides should be hung a kind of short curtain with one opening through which the chickens can run in and out. The legs on one side should be a little taller than those on the other, so that there is a space for chickens of all sizes.

The water should be kept at 110 degrees on the common or Fahrenheit thermometer. The chickens, as soon as they are thoroughly dry, should be placed under the artificial mother, and they soon learn to come out and feed, when a noise is made like the clucking or calling of a hen. The great difficulty is to keep the artificial mother of a nearly uniform temperature. This we have accomplished by a very small night-light placed under one of the angles, and separated from the chickens by a small screen of tin plate.

In using the artificial mother, care must be taken to

shift the place on which it stands every day, so as to enable the ground under it to be cleaned daily, the least accumulation of dirt being fatal to the chicken. Even with every care that can be taken, the mortality of chickens brought up in this way is much greater than that of those running with the hens. Ducks, however, are much more hardy, and can be hatched in an incubator, and reared with the artificial mother, without any difficulty.

As far as regards the raising of chickens in the winter without hens, we must candidly give our honest opinion against it. Incubators are of great use to those who wish to study the development of the chicken in the egg. They are also valuable for hatching chickens in summer when they can be reared under hens. In the Zoological Gardens they have been very useful in hatching out the eggs of rare birds, and they do well in Egypt, and other hot climates, where the chickens are not liable to be affected by cold; but as a substitute for natural means of rearing birds in this climate they will not be found to answer.

As an amusement and means of study, the incubator is very well; but no artificial mother is equal to the hen, as, though her natural warmth may be imitated, the care and assiduity with which she tends her young, and scratches to find their natural food, is beyond all imitation.

CHAPTER V.

DISEASES OF FOWLS, ETC.

FOWLS are subject to several sorts of distemper — some affecting the skin, others the lungs, the ovaries, the brain, the digestive system, and the limbs.

Skin Diseases are common among fowls kept in confined, close, or dirty yards, stables, &c. Cochins are especially subject to skin diseases if fed upon greaves and offal. Absolute cure of a bad case is, perhaps, impossible, but when the attack appears on the neck or head, a five-grain Plummer's pill every three days will sometimes prevent further mischief. But if the fowl shows no symptoms of improvement, the best thing you can do with it is to wring its neck.

Moulting must not be regarded as a disease, for it is a regular operation of nature. It consists of a gradual exchange of old feathers for new ones. "Nevertheless," says an acute observer, "it often happens that birds in a state of domestication have not sufficient vital energy for the accomplishment of the exchange. They require improved diet, warmth, and good water. Of course their roosting-place must be properly sheltered and ventilated. A grain or two of cayenne pepper, made into a pill with bread, may be given daily with advantage. Douglas's mixture, or a nail, or any bit of iron, may be put into the drinking-trough, in order to render the water chalybeate."

"*Croup*, from the similarity of its name, is often confounded with Roup, from which, however, it is perfectly distinct, being inflammation of the windpipe: the symptoms are a difficulty in breathing and a rattling or peculiar noise in the throat, this, in some cases, is even musical; sometimes thick glairy mucus is coughed up, but there is never any swelling of the face or discharge from the nostrils. The disease is most frequent in damp weather, and yields readily to warm, dry housing, and one-twelfth of a grain of tartar emetic.

" *Inflammation of the lungs* is known by a difficulty of breathing, but without the noise of croup: the same treatment with tartar emetic is advisable.

" *Consumption*, arising from the presence of scrofulous matter in the lungs, is produced by cold, damp, bad, food, and is also inherited from parents; this disease being hereditary, it is worse than useless to attempt to cure fowls that are affected, as the chickens are certain to be tainted with the disease.

" *Pip* is the name given to a dry horny scale which appears on the tongue, in all those diseases in which the fowl becomes feverish; it is only a symptom of internal fever, and not a disease itself, the remedy is to remove the real disease causing it.

" *Gapes* in chickens is caused by peculiar parasitic worms adhering to the inside of the windpipe; they are readily removed by stripping a small quill of its side feather, except an inch of the end, dipping it in spirits of turpentine, and inserting it in the windpipe; but as this remedy often excites fatal inflammation, fumigation with the vapour of turpentine, by shutting the chicken up in a box, with some shavings moistened with the spirit, as long as they can withstand the action of the vapour, has been found a very successful remedy."

Roup.—A correspondent of the " Cottage Gardener," asks for advice in case of Roup, and then states his case: " My Dorkings have been attacked with swelled heads, and eyes—in some only one eye, in others both. None of those that became wholly blind have recovered their sight, but died in a few days; most of the others are getting well, though their eyes are very weak. Their feathers look well, and, for the most part, they eat well and run about as usual. The coops are placed several yards apart on a large piece of short grass, of which the chickens have the run, and the ground is not overstocked with fowls. I have given the afflicted ones 'Bailey's roup and condition pills,' and washed their heads once or twice a day in weak vinegar and water, when a film, in some cases as thick as the white of an egg, came off the eye. I fear the disease is infectious, as a large cockerel of more than two months old has also lately been attacked, and I think will not live. Can you suggest any remedy for this disease?"

To this the Poultry Editor replies, "Remove the infected from the healthy chickens. Feed both freely on bread and ale, and let some of the earth close to their rips be turned up and over, with spade or fork, every night and morning. Your treatment of the sick chickens is right—continue washing with cold water and vinegar. Where young chickens have both eyes closed, kill them at once."

Diseases of the ovaries, which produce soft, or imperfect eggs, are cured by lime, and by a grain of calomel and tartar emetic, mixed with meal, and administered as a pill.

Cramp, leg weakness, inflammation of the feet, and bumble foot are relieved by the administration of a little iron and colchicum.

Broken wings may be repaired by tying the points of the quill feathers together in a natural position; but, after all, the safe plan when your fowls are attacked, is to kill them, and so prevent disease spreading to the rest of your stock.

"*Apoplexy*," says Miss Watts, "often makes its attack without previous warning. Could it be known that a bird was in danger, it might be reduced, physicked, or bled to insure safety. Aviary birds, in the finest health apparently, will drop dead from their perch from this cause. They are often over-fed, they have not to exercise themselves in the task of seeking for food, they have an allowance in unlimited measure, but have no according measure of muscular exertion; they 'do not earn their bread before they eat it,' as wild birds do. '*Experientia docet.*' The best advice to give as to the means of *prevention,* is to feed birds a little in proportion to the exercise which they have the power to take."

In point of economy, it is cheaper to kill than to cure diseased fowls, for in most cases these ailments do not destroy their value as food if they be got ready for the table as soon as the disease presents itself, while attempts at doctoring them often result in loss and failure. Care in the feeding and housing of fowls will generally prevent disease.

Lice, which frequent fowls, may be got rid of by dusting the bird's skin under the feathers with flour of brimstone, and keeping their houses clean with lime-wash.

Dryness of atmosphere affects fowls very much, from the absence of the animal life so necessary to their sustenance. Counteract dryness by artificial watering, and wetness by throwing dust and ashes about the birds' run. It will be found that your fowls will immediately take advantage of the change, and improve in appearance and flesh.

THE END.

www.ingramcontent.com/pod-product-compliance
Lightning Source LLC
Chambersburg PA
CBHW081241280526
45787CB00006B/2752